Dash

Dash

"What Will Your Dash Mean?"

William D. Martin

Copyright © 2009 by William D. Martin.

Library of Congress Control Number: 2009901433
ISBN: Hardcover   978-1-4415-1135-5
           Softcover   978-1-4415-1134-8

All rights reserved. No part of this book may be reproduced or transmitted in any form or by any means, electronic or mechanical, including photocopying, recording, or by any information storage and retrieval system, without permission in writing from the copyright owner.

This book was printed in the United States of America.

To order additional copies of this book, contact:
Xlibris Corporation
1-888-795-4274
www.Xlibris.com
Orders@Xlibris.com

Contents

Introduction 9

Chapter One   Being at Cause 13

Chapter Two   Purpose 17

Chapter Three   Plan 22

Chapter Four   Picture 33

Chapter Five   People 44

Chapter Six   Renewal 53

Summary 55

Additional Forms 57

Your Dash

On the day of your death, you will be buried beneath a tombstone that contains your name, the date of your birth, and the date of your death. Separating your birth and death dates is but a single dash—a dash that represents everything about the life you chose to lead.

It represents who you were as a person.
It represents what you were all about.
It represents the things you did and didn't do in your life.
It represents the impact of your life on the world around you.
It represents everything about the life you chose to live.

When all is said and done, what will your dash mean?
This book is a guide to making your dash mean what you want it to mean and to create the life you want it to represent.

Introduction

Go confidently in the direction of your dreams.
Live the life you have imagined.
—Henry David Thoreau

If you can imagine it, you can achieve it; if you can dream it,
you can become it.
—William Arthur Ward

The objective of this book is to provide you with the tools necessary to take control of your life, create your future, and surround yourself with the people and contacts necessary to achieve your life goals. It is designed to make your dash the life you choose it to be. It has been said that many people spend more time planning their vacations than they do their lives. As a result, they fall into the trap of letting life happen to them rather than creating the life that they want. Living this way is called being at effect. At-effect people accept the life that is given to them by their environment. However, other people choose to actively guide and influence their lives to create the future they want. This is called being at cause. At-cause people choose to influence their environment and create the life they want to have. Successful people have a mindset toward life that is at cause. Being at cause is the first of the five critical elements necessary to create the future you desire. The five critical elements are the following:

Being at cause. Are you happening to life or is life happening to you? What is your mindset toward life? Are you living the life you want or living a life based on the expectations of others? Do you view life as something to be shaped and guided, or is it something that simply happens that you cannot control? Recognizing that as they move through life there are things that they can influence and things they cannot, at-cause people choose to influence the things in their world that will make their life better. They respond to situations, even negative ones, in a positive way that looks at their choices and takes responsibility for their actions. At-effect people choose not to influence their environment. They react to situations, especially negative ones, in a negative way that places blame on others or the situation. In this way, they avoid taking responsibility or making choices, but sacrifice influence over their lives. Successful people assume an at-cause mindset toward life and create the life they desire.

Purpose. Ask yourself, "Why am I here? What is my reason for being? What is my purpose on this earth?" Successful people have a strong sense of personal purpose. The answers to these questions help reveal your personal purpose for being. Personal purpose provides direction and guides your choices for the future much like a compass always lets you know which way is north.

Plan. Where are you going? In order to create your future, you need goals and a plan that is aligned with your personal purpose. The plan needs to balance each aspect of your life. If one of the aspects of your life is out of balance, it impacts all the others. Many people struggle with work/life balance. What they are really struggling with is overall life balance. Work is only a part of the overall bigger picture.

Successful people have a balanced life plan that is aligned with their personal purpose.

Picture. Who do you believe you are? What is your picture of yourself? What do you believe you can or cannot do? Everyone has a picture of themselves that they have been creating since they were born. It is your self-image. It is filled with your beliefs about yourself. It is your overall evaluation of you. What you believe you are good at and what you believe you are not good at. How you see yourself physically and intellectually. In order to accomplish your purpose and life plan, you must believe you are capable of accomplishing it.

People. Who knows you? Who you know is not as important as who knows you. Everyone has a personal network. Who is in yours? What's the quality of each relationship? Who is helping you achieve your goals and who is not? Who is not in your network that should be? Who might you need to sever relationships with? Successful people manage their network of relationships to increase their social capital, thus opening avenues to communication, exposure, and opportunities. Successful people surround themselves with people that are supportive and helpful to achieving their life plan and purpose.

If you complete the exercises in this book, you will emerge with the following:

- Being at cause
- A clear purpose for your life
- A clear plan outlining your goals and a plan to achieve them
- An understanding of your current self-image
- A clear definition of the self-image you desire and a plan to achieve it
- A clear definition of your current social network

- A clear definition of your desired social network
- A plan for renewal

The model is quite simple.

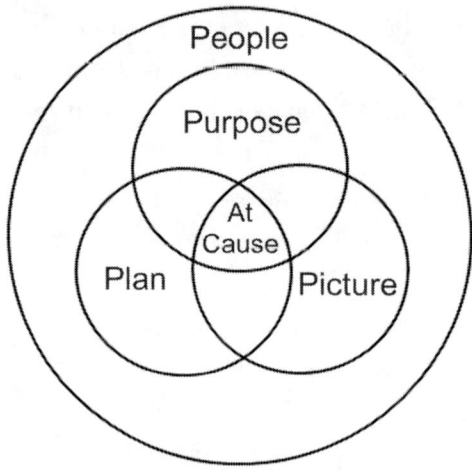

At Cause: Choosing to happen to life rather than letting life happen to you
Purpose: Having a clear purpose for your life
Plan: Knowing where you are I going and what is my plan to get there
Picture: Having a picture of yourself that will help you succeed
People: Surrounding yourself with people that will help you reach your dreams

At the completion of this book, you will have a powerful plan to achieve your dreams and define what your dash will mean.

Chapter One

Being at Cause

There are three types of people in this world: those who make things happen, those who watch things happen and those who wonder what happened. We all have a choice. You can decide which type of person you want to be. I have always chosen to be in the first group.
—Mary Kay Ash

Nothing can stop the man with the right mental attitude from achieving his goal; nothing on earth can help the man with the wrong mental attitude.
—Thomas Jefferson

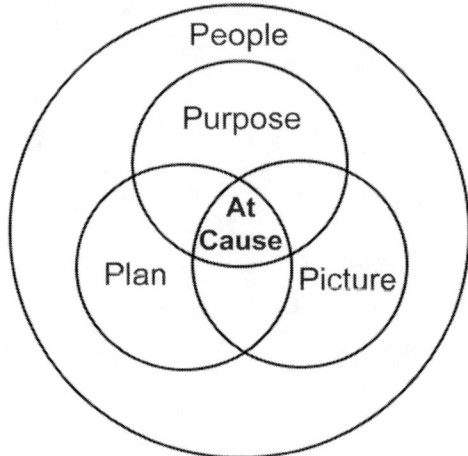

There is a wise Indian prayer that states, "God, grant me the serenity to accept the things I cannot change, the courage to change the things I can, and the wisdom to know the difference." As time goes by, there are things that you can influence and things that you cannot.

Being at cause does not mean that you adopt an irrational belief that you can control everything. What it does mean is taking responsibility for your own life. At-cause people choose to influence the things they can to make their lives better. It is a mental state of defining options and making choices to guide and influence your future. At-cause people respond positively even to a negative situation and quickly start to identify their choices and alternatives. This then allows them to influence their environment and continue to maintain control of their lives. At-cause people happen to life.

At-effect people choose not to take responsibility for their lives. They will assume a helpless-victim mentality, placing blame on others or the external situation. "The reason I did poorly in school was my teacher." "The reason I did poorly in my job was my boss." "There was nothing I could do." At-effect people frequently will engage in a game called "Ain't that awful!" "Ain't it awful what they are doing?" "Ain't it awful how bad it is?" Since they do not identify choices or ways of influencing their environment for the future, they tend to have little or no control over future events. In essence, they shift the power to control their lives from themselves to the environment, creating a self-fulfilling prophecy. At-effect people let life happen to them.

Whether you are at cause or at effect, the reality is what actually happens, happens. Once a situation has taken place, it is what it is. The question is then "How do you choose to respond to it?" Do you choose to respond to the situation from an "at-cause" or an "at-effect" mindset?

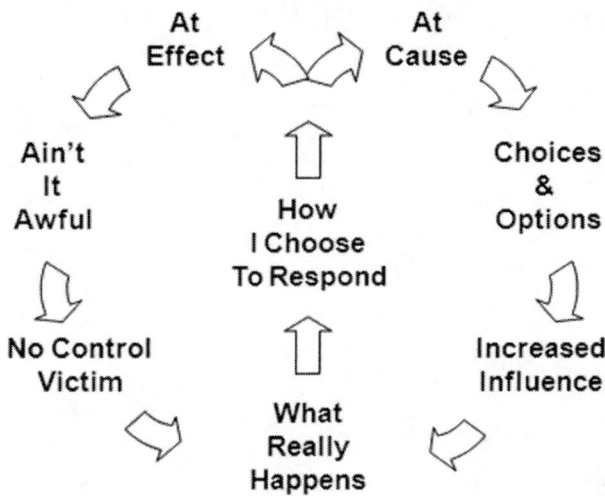

At-cause people assess the situation, determine their choices and options, and begin to move in the direction that provide them the best life. This increases their influence over future events. This can result in new options and choices over time. It is a continual process of defining my choices now, choosing the best one, and moving on.

At-effect people give their power away to the environment and don't identify their choices. They blame the environment and assume a victim mentality, which decreases their influence over their lives and future events. They tend not to move on but stay stuck waiting for the environment to dictate their future. At-effect people wait for life to happen to them and trade success for the comfort of avoiding responsibility for their lives. Since they do not take control of their life, they lose the ability to influence it and see themselves as having no control.

Successful people assume an at-cause mindset. They happen to life. They define options and choices that allow them to create their future. This allows them to be the architect of their life and future. They chart a course to create their own destiny. What mindset have you been choosing? What mindset will you choose now? If you really want to choose being at cause as a way of life, then make this promise to yourself and sign your name and date it.

"I choose to live an at-cause life from this day forth."

Your signature _____

Date ____/____/____

Chapter Two

Purpose

To be yourself in a world that is constantly trying to make you something else is the greatest accomplishment.
—Ralph Waldo Emerson

Many people have a wrong idea of what constitutes true happiness. It is not attained through self-gratification, but through fidelity to a worthy purpose.
—Helen Keller

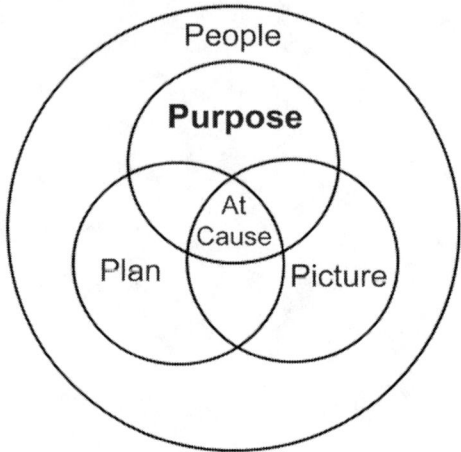

For centuries, people have pondered the question "What is the meaning of life?" The nature of the question implies that there is one single meaning or purpose we all share. This purpose can and should be discovered if one searches hard enough. It also implies that that meaning is somewhere outside of ourselves.

If you challenge these assumptions, a different way to think about the meaning of life is to consider that each life has a unique meaning and purpose found inside ourselves. There is no one single purpose of life but a tapestry of unique purposes that, gathered together, creates a whole. It is not something to be discovered outside of ourselves but rather something discovered within that we choose for ourselves. This means that the meaning of life is what I choose it to be.

The implication of this way of thinking is profound. If the meaning of life comes from inside our self rather than from somewhere outside our self, it implies that we are responsible for the meaning and purpose of our own life. It means that instead of letting life just happen to us, we are responsible for creating the life that we want.

This way of thinking brings up a whole different set of questions to be answered. "What do you choose to be the meaning of your life?" "What do you choose as your purpose for being?"

One factor that separates successful people from unsuccessful people is having a strong sense of purpose. Personal purpose provides direction and guides your choices for the future. It forces you to think deeply about your life and to be clear about what is really important to you. It becomes your personal compass to guide you through good times and bad.

Defining your personal purpose begins with introspection. It is as much an act of discovery as it is an act of creation. It is determining what is really important to you. The following questions are designed to assist in the personal discovery process of defining what is truly important to you.

> What are the five most important things in your life?
> What are the things you have done in your life that have given you the most satisfaction?
> What do you want from your life?
> What would you like to say you've accomplished at the end of your life?
> What do you stand for in life?
> What are the things you would fight for?
> What are you passionate about?
> What are the things in your life that have given you the most satisfaction?

As you think about your answers to these questions, you may find common themes. Most people do. These common themes form the basis for your personal purpose in life. Your personal purpose is your statement about what you are about. Based on your answers to the questions above, what is your unique purpose on this earth that captures the essence of your being and evokes your passion? Take a moment and draft your personal purpose statement.

Note that it does not have to be perfect the first time as this is the start of a work in progress. As you pass through time, you will want to revisit your purpose for several reasons. The first reason is to determine whether or not you are living by it. The second reason is to reevaluate it against your world at that moment. As life changes take place, you may find that there are things about your purpose that need to be added or modified. A life-change example would be becoming a parent or caregiver. You will also find that some things are just fine as they are. Your personal purpose should provide strong direction but be adaptable to life's changes.

I choose my unique purpose in life to be

_____

_____

_____

It is sometimes helpful to condense your personal purpose into a simplified motto or slogan. It should be something memorable that will keep your purpose alive and in the front of your mind when you speak it. For instance, it could say, "If I had a motto or slogan that would capture my purpose in one short tag line, it would be . . ."

_____

Now that you have decided on your unique reason for being, you can then look at how it plays out in the different roles you play in life. Each of us plays a number of roles in our lives, and we assume different roles over time. We all start as children. Some of us become parents. We are children to our parents. Some of us will get married. You can expand your personal purpose to include these roles in your life to provide clarity about how your purpose manifests itself in different ways. Here are a few examples:

I am Father

I am father to my children and, as such, I am their living example of how to be. I am their coach, their janitor, their policeman, counselor, and friend. My job is to help each of them to become the best person they can be and realize their true potential. I am to help them learn how to handle life in the best way they know how.

I am Son

I am my parents' son, and as such, I have a responsibility to honor and help them as they have done for me. I need to consider how I behave as I move from the stage of being cared for to the stage of caregiver. As their health submits to the weathering of age, I need to contribute to their comfort in ways that preserves their dignity.

I am Me

I am me, the employee and citizen, and as such, I have a responsibility to conduct myself in ways that are consistent with my values and beliefs. I influence those around me through my actions and my behaviors. I need to be the change I want to see in the world.

There are other roles such as wife/husband, sister/brother, coach, stepmother, member of the community, and others. Every life assumes different roles over time, which is why a personal purpose must be a continual work in progress, one that is renewed to reflect the reality of life as it changes.

Once you have established your personal purpose, you have answered the question "Why am I here?" This provides the foundation for the next question and next part of the model "Where am I going?"

Chapter Three

Plan

A good plan is like a road map: it shows the final destination and usually the best way to get there.
—H. Stanley Judd

Without goals, and plans to reach them, you are like a ship that has set sail with no destination.
—Fitzhugh Dodson

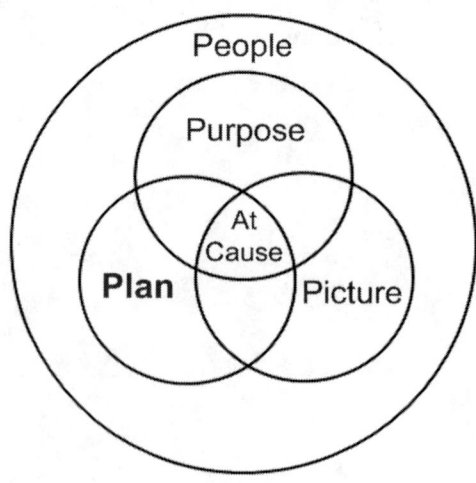

It has been said that people spend more time planning their vacations than they do their lives. You only get one life. What happens between birth and death is up to you.

The Big Picture

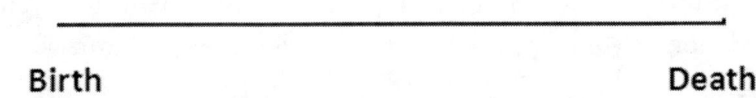

Birth — Death

You are somewhere on the timeline between birth and death. No one knows just how long their timeline will be. What has taken place is gone. You cannot go back and change it. You can only focus on the part of your life yet to be determined. The question is "What are you going to do with it?"

The Big Picture

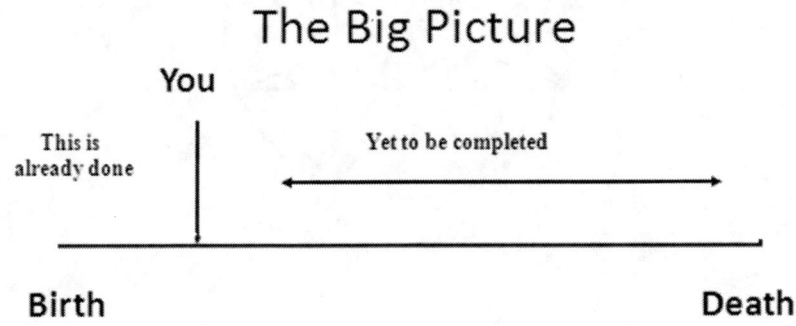

In the book *Alice in Wonderland,* Alice has a discussion with a Cheshire cat. It goes something like this:

> "Would you tell me, please, which way I ought to go from here?" said Alice.
> "That depends a good deal on where you want to get to," said the cat.

"I don't much care where," said Alice.
"Then it doesn't matter which way you go," said the cat.

The brilliance in this discussion is that it highlights the notion that if you know where you want to go, you have a much higher chance of getting there than if you don't. Without some kind of direction, you will get somewhere, but it may not be where you want to be when you arrive.

That is where life planning comes in. Life planning is a way to create a balanced life plan to achieve your goals over time. Now that you have the foundation of your personal purpose, it is time to look at where you are going.

Life planning looks at eight areas:

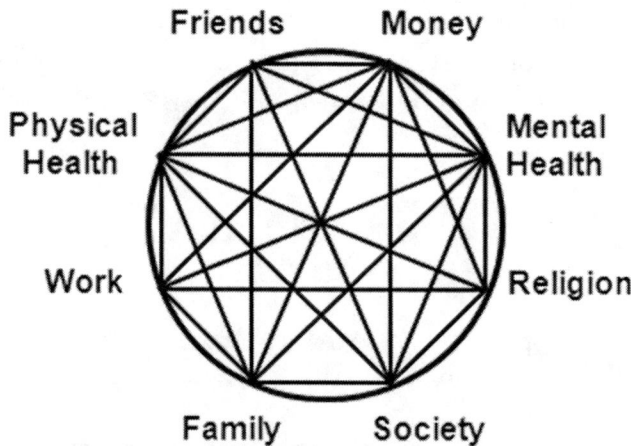

These areas are not exclusive but rather are interdependent upon each other. If any one of these areas goes out of balance, it will throw the others out of balance as well. Picture in your mind rubber bands connecting each of the elements shown above. Then picture pulls on one of the elements. You would feel tension as you pulled. That is the tension of being out of balance. As one element goes out of balance, it directly impacts the others.

For example, if you have a family problem, it can have an adverse impact on any of the other elements in your life. Many people are feeling a pull from the work element that can create issues with physical health and family, to name a few.

To create a balanced life plan, you need to make challenging, but achievable goals in each one of these areas. This assures attention is paid to each area, which creates a balancing effect.

The first step in creating your plan is to do an assessment of your starting position. Take a moment and evaluate your personal situation with regard to each area by placing an *X* on the scale where you feel each element is now from "needs improvement" to "is in excellent shape."

	Needs Improvement	Neutral	Excellent
Physical	(-)	-/+	(+)
Mental	(-)	-/+	(+)
Family	(-)	-/+	(+)
Friends	(-)	-/+	(+)
Money	(-)	-/+	(+)
Work	(-)	-/+	(+)
Religion	(-)	-/+	(+)
Society	(-)	-/+	(+)

Look at the overall balance in your life. As you look at the balance in your life, where do you see opportunities for you to grow? Where is there tension that is pulling you out of balance? What are the areas where you would like to achieve significant improvement?

The next question is "What are you going to do about it?"

The next exercise is designed to develop a balanced one-year life plan.

For each area listed on the following page, identify three challenging, achievable, and desirable things you want to accomplish by New Year's eve of this year. These are goals you are setting for yourself to take control for the "yet to be determined" part of your timeline. They don't have to be perfect or monumental. They need to be things that you choose to be a part of your future. Over the course of the year, you can revisit them and refine them. New goals can be added and existing ones modified as time goes by. The key is that you are now laying out your life plan for your future.

My physical health goals

1.

2.

3.

My mental health goals

1.

2.

3.

My family life goals

1.

2.

3.

My friends/social life goals

1.

2.

3.

My money goals

1.

2.

3.

My work life goals

1.

2.

3.

My religious life goals

1.

2.

3.

My society/community life goals

1.

2.

3.

This becomes your balanced plan for this year. As you might imagine, once you know what you want to accomplish, it is only a matter of taking steps to do it. Use the space below to identify the first three actions you will take in order to begin making your dreams come true.

1. _____

2. _____

3. _____

The next step is to broaden the time horizon to three years or more. In the next three to five years, what would you like to say you have accomplished on New Year's eve in each of these areas?

My physical health goals

1.

2.

3.

My mental health goals

1.

2.

3.

My family life goals

1.

2.

3.

My friends/social life goals

1.

2.

3.

My money goals

1.

2.

3.

My work life goals

1.

2.

3.

My religious life goals

1.

2.

3.

My society/community life goals

1.

2.

3.

Use the space below to identify the first three actions you will take in order to begin making your dreams come true.

1. _____

2. _____

3. _____

At this point, you should have an understanding of what it means to be "at cause." You have defined your personal purpose and now have a life plan to begin taking control of your future. Don't worry if it is not perfect. Consider it a work in progress that can be improved over time. The next step is to assess your picture of yourself as you have painted it.

Chapter Four

Picture

Don't limit yourself. Many people limit themselves to what they think they can do. You can go as far as your mind lets you. What you believe, you can achieve.
—Mary Kay Ash

To accomplish great things, we must not only act, but also dream, not only plan, but also believe.
—Anatole France

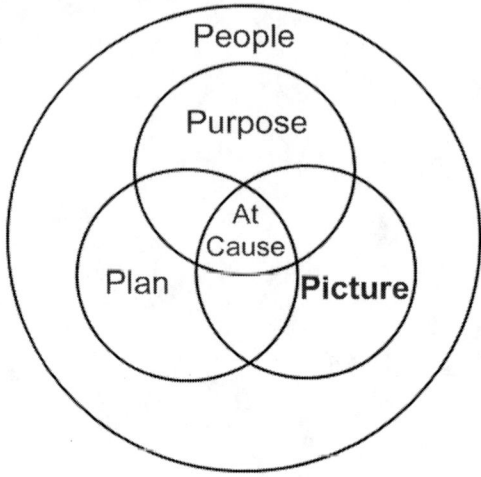

Who do you believe you are? What is your picture of yourself? What do you believe you can or cannot do? Everyone has a picture of themselves that they have been creating since they were born. It is your self-image. It is filled with your beliefs about yourself. It is your overall evaluation of you. What you believe you are good at and what you believe you are not good at. How you think about yourself physically and intellectually. In order to accomplish your purpose and life plan, you must believe you are capable of accomplishing it.

Have you ever been to the circus and seen an elephant tied to a little wooden stake in the ground? Have you ever wondered how such a tiny little stake can keep a powerful animal like an elephant from simply walking away? The truth is the elephant could walk away. The elephant simply doesn't believe it can. When a baby elephant is being domesticated, their foot is tied to a metal stake with a strong chain. The metal stake is secured in concrete, deep in the ground. When the elephant tries to pull away, it trips and falls. After a while, the elephant learns that the stake is immovable. Once that belief is established, the elephant will no longer try to pull away and a smaller wooden stake can be used in its place. The elephant is now no longer held captive by the stake itself but rather by the elephant's own belief. This represents the power beliefs have on our behavior. If you believe you can, or you believe you can't, you are usually right.

It has been said that a child comes into the world with a clean slate. Upon this slate or canvas, you begin to paint a picture of yourself, the world, and others as you know them and believe them to be true.

This chapter focuses on the part of that picture that represents you as you know you and believe you to be true. This picture is your self-image, and you have been painting it since the day you were born and will continue to paint it until the day you die.

At first, your canvas is blank so your picture could turn out to be anything. The first brushstrokes came when you arrived in this world although you probably weren't aware of it. Simple things like how you were held, the funny noises people feel compelled to make to babies, whether the doctor spanked you, how people reacted to you, all cast initial brushstrokes on your canvas. Each of these things provided you your initial information about you. Most of these were provided to you because your ability to think and comprehend was relatively rudimentary and, quite honestly, you slept a lot.

However, as you grew older and became more consciously aware of yourself and your surroundings, your role in picking and choosing the strokes to be painted also grew. Information was presented to you from your environment and you had to decide what to do with it. You began to have more control over what things from that environment you accepted to be true about yourself and what things you didn't. You began to compare what was being presented to you to the picture you already had of yourself to see which new brushstrokes complemented your picture and which ones did not.

Said another way, in the beginning, the brushstrokes provided from the environment influenced the picture but over time, the picture began to influence the brushstrokes accepted from the environment.

The result is that at any particular moment in time, your picture of you is your picture at that moment.

Your picture of you defines for you your basic beliefs about yourself. It is your internal self-portrait of you:

- How you believe you appear to others
- How you see yourself physically and athletically
- How you see yourself intellectually
- What skills and abilities you believe you are good or bad at
- Whether you see yourself as better than, equal to, or less than others
- How you relate to others
- What kind of person you think you are
- Whether you are a happy or sad person
- Whether you see yourself as a good or bad person

There are many facets to your painting.

How does your picture affect you? Your picture represents your beliefs about yourself. And you will behave in ways that are consistent with your values and beliefs.

There are parts of your picture that will benefit you and lead you to success. However, there may be parts of your picture that can lead you to failure or that will sabotage your goals.

For example, if you believe you are good at math and you are presented with a math problem to solve, you may see it as an exciting challenge to apply your skills. However, if you believe you are not good at math, then you may see the same math problem as a threat. This can turn into a self-fulfilling prophecy. Your belief that you are good at something will cause you to do it more frequently and like it more. You will then develop increasing skill and reinforce your belief that you are good at it. However, the negative belief that you are not good at math may cause you to avoid it and develop no new skill, reinforcing the belief that you are not good at math. So in a sense, our thoughts create our reality!

We are presented with thousands of potential brushstrokes on a daily basis from family, friends, television, advertising, and many other influences. We tend to accept brushstrokes that match our existing picture over those that do not. This is more comfortable because we have already accepted the previous brushstrokes as true. Information that challenges our picture can cause conflict even if it challenges a negative belief, so it may be discounted, ignored, or modified to fit the existing picture. However, it is the negative parts of our picture that do not help us that we must challenge.

This becomes very important to understand, especially with regard to achieving your purpose and plan. In order to accomplish your purpose and plan, you must believe you can accomplish them. Otherwise, you could actually sabotage yourself and not even know it.

The key is to realize that your picture or self-image changes over time. Your self-image in kindergarten, middle school, high school, and today has developed and changed over time as more and more brushstrokes have been added. It changes by adding new brushstrokes slowly over time, or it can change rapidly based on significant emotional events such as a birth, death, significant success, failure, or possibly injury. You are constantly painting or repainting portions based on new self-awareness.

What most people do not realize is that once they know about their picture, they can choose to be at cause or at effect about it. Your picture is being painted even as you read this book. The question is whether you choose to consciously take control of the painting or leave it to fate.

You can take control of your picture of yourself and align it toward being successful at your mission and your plan.

For example, a young woman started walking to get into shape. She had worked up to three miles when presented with the opportunity to do an eight-mile walk around Mackinac Island. Her original belief was "I could never do eight miles." However, she tried and was successful. All of a sudden, eight miles was no longer unachievable but was a "piece of cake." Her belief about her ability to walk long distances changed from this event as she added a big new brushstroke to her canvas. She then thought that if she could do eight miles, then she could probably do a half marathon, which is thirteen and one-tenth miles. She had now set a goal and began to train for a half marathon. She signed up and successfully completed the half marathon in less than three hours. A big new brushstroke was added to her canvas. As you can imagine, the next goal was to complete a full marathon, which she went on to do in six and a half hours.

This is an outstanding example of how beliefs and goals work. Had this woman let the initial belief "I could never do eight miles" stop her, she would have never completed a full marathon. Instead, she challenged the belief, set a goal, and put into action a plan. When she realized that she was going to accomplish the goal, the old belief was painted over with a new belief. The new belief has now been proven and has become fact.

There are several steps for taking control of your picture. The first step is to identify the things contained within your picture that will help you achieve your purpose and plan. The second step is to identify the thing contained within your picture that will hinder you from achieving your goals. The third step is to put a plan in place to leverage the things that will help you and to repaint over the negative parts of your picture with your new brushstrokes.

The questions below are divided into two categories, doing and being. Beliefs about things you believe you can or cannot do and beliefs about you as a person.

What are the things that I know I can *do* right now that will help me move toward my purpose and goals? How can I capitalize on these things to move me toward my goals?

What are things that I *believe about myself* that will help me move toward my purpose and goals? How can I capitalize on these beliefs to move me toward my goals?

What are the *skills or abilities I need to develop* or find someone to help me with in order to move toward my purpose and goals? What can I do to begin developing these skills and abilities?

What are things I *believe about myself* that might hinder me from moving toward my purpose and goals? What can I do to challenge these beliefs and replace them with new beliefs that will move me toward my goals?

Once you have identified the things in your self-image picture that you want to either leverage, develop, or change about yourself, you can then develop a change plan. For example, you decide on a goal to start a retirement account.

Things you decide you can do right now are as follows:

- Define your current expenses
- Define your income stream
- Define your assets and liabilities
- Look for classes on retirement accounts at the community college
- Research companies that specialize in retirement accounts
- Determine how much money you have available to invest

Things you believe about yourself that will help you achieve your goals:

- You are a smart person
- You manage money well
- You are a responsible person
- You learn fast

Skills and abilities you need to develop:

- Learn how the stock market works
- Learn about mutual funds
- Learn the rules of retirement accounts
- Learn basic economics

How you plan to develop them:

- Take courses at the local community college
- Check out books on stocks and mutual funds at the library
- Go to a retirement symposium

Beliefs about yourself that need to be challenged:

- You do not believe you are good at math

How you decide to challenge that belief:

- You decide today that you are going to become good at math and will do so by taking math classes
- You are going to check out math books at the library
- You are going to explore what learning tools are available on the Web

You can see that many of these things are also things that should become part of your life plan in addition to being on your self-image plan. The important thing is, you are taking positive action to move toward your goals and purpose and you are not letting any self-imposed barriers prevent your success.

There is one more piece of your self-image picture that is important to address in order to eliminate self-sabotage. I call it the voices in your head.

What are the voices in your head? Everyone engages in a form of self-talk. Things that you say to yourself that no one else hears. In the movie *What Women Want*, Mel Gibson is in the bathroom and accidentally slips on some bath beads. The hairdryer falls into the tub while he still has one foot in, jolting him with electricity. The next day, he wakes up and finds he can hear women's innermost thoughts. He is able to hear their internal dialogue, which is the basis of the movie. This innermost dialogue is called self-talk.

So what are you saying to you about you? Are you saying things to yourself that are helpful or hurtful to achieving your goals? Self-talk tends to reinforce existing beliefs about you. Therefore, you will say positive things about the things you believe you do well. You will tend to say negative things about the things you do not believe you do well. If you want to change negative beliefs about yourself, then you must change your inner dialogue to prevent it from sabotaging you.

Take our example above. If you do not believe you are good at math, then you might say things like "Math is hard. I never did do math well. I hate math." This kind of self-talk is reinforcing the negative belief "I am not good at math." This kind of self-talk might cause you to not act on the items you listed above.

However, this is the belief you have decided to change. Therefore, you need to change your inner dialogue to something that reinforces the new belief you have chosen for yourself. This can be done through something called positive affirmations. An affirmation is a positive statement that has been specifically worded for the purpose of reprogramming the subconscious mind with positive thoughts. It is one of the key tools for changing beliefs you have about yourself. This is a fundamental tool given that our thoughts create our reality!

What is amazing is your mind does not distinguish between intentionally self-programmed affirmation and actual self-talk. Consider an athlete faced with the challenge of a large hill to run up at the end of a marathon. Consider how their mind and body would react if the athlete engages in negative self-talk such as "I hurt. I feel awful. My legs feel like jelly. That's a huge hill." How well do you think they would do? However, many marathon runners have positive affirmations they repeat to themselves when faced with a challenge. Consider how the athlete's performance would be different if they said things like "I feel good, I am strong, and I am going to do this. It's just a little hill, but I've seen bigger." Coaches frequently will program athletes to engage in nothing but positive self-talk as it improves their performance considerably.

Affirmations stated over and over many times can become fact to the brain, especially when supported by positive events from your life and self-image plan. For example, in our self-image example plan, the negative belief that was chosen to be changed was "I am not good at math." The counteraffirmation would be either "I am going to get good at math" or "I am good at math." Said over and over again, it challenges the old self-talk. If you signed up for classes and studied hard, you might receive an A on your first test. This is now factual reinforcement of the new belief.

Given the belief(s) you desire to change about yourself, create a list of affirmations that you will commit to say to yourself each morning before starting your day and each night before you go to bed. The more frequently you say them, the bigger the impact they will have on you. You will also want to add to your list affirmations that continually reinforce those beliefs that are helping you achieve your goals. Using our retirement example, some affirmations might be the following:

> I am a smart person.
> I manage money well.
> I am a responsible person.
> I learn fast.
> I am good at math.
> I can learn math because I am a smart, responsible person.

Notice that each affirmation begins with the word *I*. Also notice that the last affirmation is built on two of the previous affirmations that I have already concluded to be true.

Take your answers to the questions on the previous pages and create at least five positive affirmations for yourself.

1.

2.

3.

4.

5.

You do not have to limit yourself to five but by writing at least five, you have a good start toward ensuring a good fit between your personal picture, your purpose, and your life plan.

Chapter Five

People

We are caught in an inescapable network of mutuality, tied in a single garment of destiny. Whatever affects one directly, affects all indirectly.
—Martin Luther King, Jr.

The quality of your life is dependent upon the quality of your relationships.
—Anthony Robbins

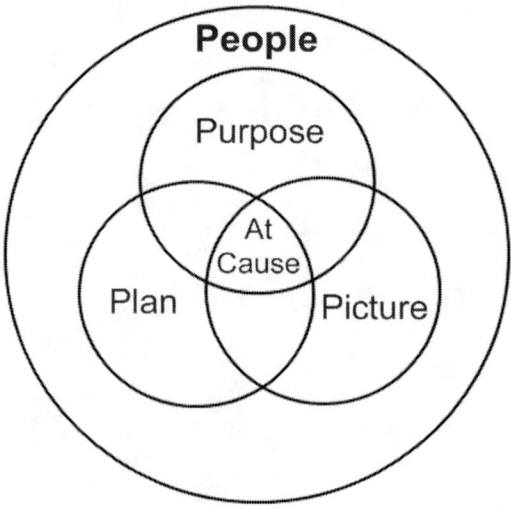

People want to succeed. However, some succeed more than others. Some succeed faster than others. Why? What causes two equally talented people to succeed at different rates to different levels of success? The truth is, there are a lot of factors that can influence a person's success. In the previous chapters, we have discussed three—having a clear and compelling purpose, plan, and picture. One additional powerful factor is social capital. Social capital is a powerful, yet covert factor that influences a person's ability to succeed. It has been said that it is not what you know but whom you know that creates success. While this is partially true, a better way to describe social capital is it is what you know, who knows you, and what is the quality of the relationships within your social network.

What is social capital, and why should you care about it? The central premise of social capital is that relationship networks have value. Social capital is an advantage one gains or loses through the quality of their relationships in their relationship network. It has also been described as the advantage created by the resources in an individual's relationship network that can be drawn on to achieve success. It is firmly rooted in the concept of reciprocity or mutual exchange for mutual benefit.

Social capital explains how some people can achieve greater success through higher quality relationships with other well-networked people. Successful people's social networks tend to have a higher collective value and inclination to cooperate than less successful people's networks do.

Social capital consists of several elements:

1. Your actual relationship network
2. The quality of your relationships within your relationship network
3. Your cultural compatibility
4. What you bring to the party

These elements in turn influence the following:

1. Your access to information flow, ideas, and knowledge
2. Your access to financial resources

3. Your credibility and legitimacy
4. Your access to influence and power
5. Availability to opportunities and leads
6. Your understanding of appropriate cultural etiquette

This leads to increased cooperation, the ability to influence, and access to opportunities that directly impact your success as a person.

Many people understand the concept of social capital as whom you know but generally see it as something that happens by luck or lineage. This book presents social capital as an overt concept rather than a covert one. As a result, it is something that can be actively managed and improved. By improving your social capital, you can dramatically increase your ability to succeed. It is important to realize when assessing your relationship network that it is more important who knows you than whom you know.

What is your current social capital? To begin assessing your social capital, you need to look at your actual relationship network. What is your personal relationship network? Who is in your personal relationship network? What is the quality of each relationship? Shown below is a typical twelve-person, personal-relationship network.

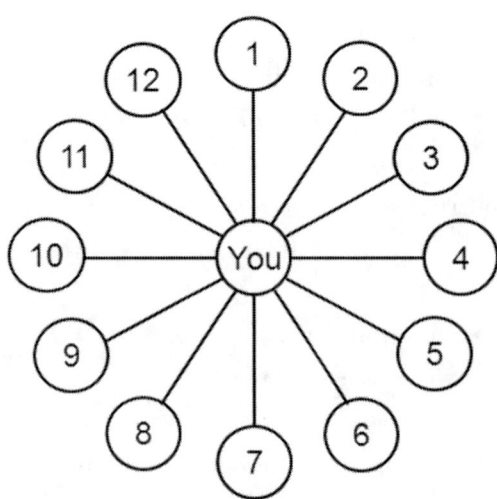

As you can see, you are in the middle of a relationship network with lines representing the relationship to each person. To begin to assess your network, take a pencil and paper and draw your own relationship network similar to the one shown above.

The next step in assessing your social capital is to objectively rate the quality of each relationship. Things to consider when evaluating the quality of your relationships are as follows:

1. The level of honesty
2. The level of trust
3. Mutuality of respect
4. Level of reciprocity
5. Cultural compatibility (class, behavioral norms, etiquettes)

As you think of each relationship in your personal relationship network and the factors listed above, you need to make an assessment of the overall quality, using the scale shown below:

Rating Definition

Rating	Definition
-1 Poor	The relationship is poor, draining, and subversive to your success.
0 New	The relationship is new and its quality yet to be determined.
1 Fair	The relationship is fair but adds little or nothing toward your success.
2 Good	The relationship is good and is helpful to your achieving success.
3 Excellent	The relationship is excellent and is very helpful to your achieving success.

Using our twelve-person network, here is what a simple assessment might look like:

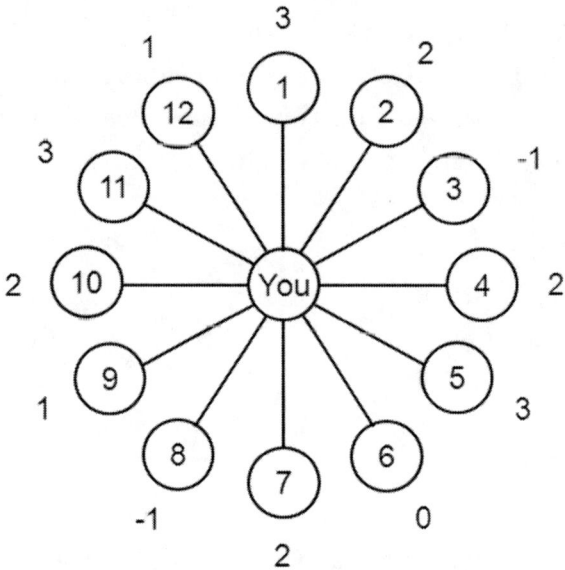

To determine the actual value of your social capital, simply add up the total. In this case, the total value of our example network would be 17. However, the potential of this network is much higher. If all twelve relationships were rated as level 3, then the potential social capital would be 36. This means that this network is only delivering 47 percent of its potential. The higher the value of your personal-relationship network, the greater success you will have toward your purpose and plan.

It is important to realize that your relationship network may cross over numerous cultures. These can be social cultures, country cultures, or business cultures. For the quality of a relationship to thrive, you need to become cognizant of the culture of the other person and behave in ways that are consistent with their culture. For example, if you were to be the new lawyer in a small town, it would be important to understand the unwritten rules of how things are done in the legal community, what is considered to be good etiquette and what is considered to be bad. If you work with small and large corporations, it is important to understand how they do business and what is okay or not okay to do. If you work internationally, understanding the etiquette of business is critical for successful business relationships.

By making your relationship network overt and assessing each relationship, you can start to manage your network. Using the table below, you can begin creating a plan to improve your personal-network value. This plan may include actions to improve highly rated relationships and to possibly sever others that are of lower value.

Rating	Questions to ask:	Actions I will take:
For those rated 3	How do I maintain the high relationship quality and not let the quality fall to a lower rating?	
For those rated 2	How do I improve these relationships from a 2 rating to a 3? What things can I do to invest in these relationships in order to improve their quality?	
For those rated 1	These relationships, by definition, are fair and not contributing to your success. They may, however, be consuming time and energy for little gain that could be spent elsewhere for greater gain. Is the investment in these relationships likely to result in a rise to a rating of a 2 or 3, or are they likely to remain at a rating of 1? This should identify ones to keep or cut loose.	

For those rated 0	These relationships, by definition, are new and unproven. What do I need to do to determine if they are ones I will add to my personal network? What is my assessment of them becoming a 2 or 3?	
For those rated -1	These relationships, by definition, are dragging you down. Are they redeemable? Should I cut them loose? If I cannot completely cut them loose, for whatever reason, how can I minimize the impact of them on my success?	

Once you have determined your personal relationship network, assessed its value, and made choices about its composition, you are ready to move on to the next step. Who is not in your personal relationship network that you believe will be important to your success? Who do you want or need to add?

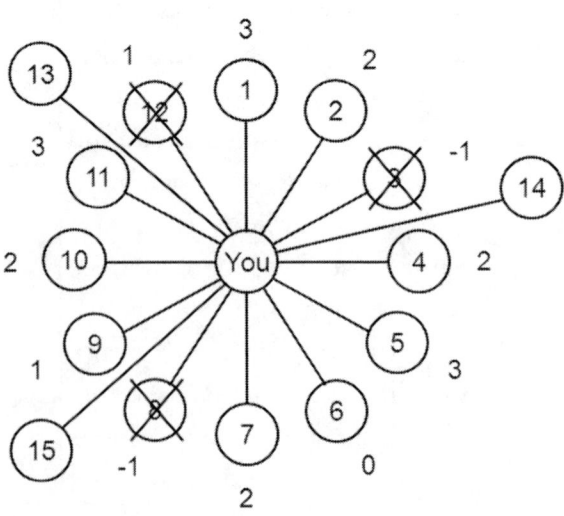

You can see by the graphic above that a choice has been made about individuals 3, 8, and 12. They offer little value or cannot be redeemed and are therefore cut loose from the relationship network. Individuals 13, 14, and 15 have been identified as new people that should be added who will add value to the relationship network.

As new members, they are rated at 0 when they join. Using the table below, identify actions you will take to build a strong relationship with the new people you desire to add to your personal network.

How will I introduce myself?	
What do I bring to offer to the relationship?	
What formal organizations do these individuals belong to that I may choose to join?	
What will attract them to me as someone that they would choose to add to their personal-relationship network?	
What things do we have in common?	
What things do they like to do?	

Using this methodology for managing your personal relationship network, you are making the covert overt and therefore you are actively improving your personal social capital from an at-cause standpoint.

As your social capital rises, so does your success toward achieving your personal purpose and plan. By creating a strong relationship network around you, you increase your access to information, ideas, and knowledge. You increase your access to financial resources. Your credibility and legitimacy increases, leading to a greater ability to influence people and to take advantage of opportunities.

Remember, a healthy-relationship network is dependent upon mutuality so you should always contribute to the success of the people in your relationship network as much if not more than they do to yours in order to keep it healthy.

Chapter Six

Renewal

> *Dreams are renewable, no matter what our age or condition.*
> —Dale E. Turner

> *Nature renews itself annually; we call them seasons.*
> —William D. Martin

Being able to continually succeed year after year requires assessment and renewal. As time goes by and you achieve your goals, or the world around you changes, it becomes important to renew your purpose and plans. At a minimum, renewal should take place every six to twelve months. At that time, you simply follow the same process you used to establish your purpose and plans. Questions to ask are the following:

1. What things are still relevant?
2. What things are not relevant anymore?
3. What things have you accomplished that should be celebrated?
4. What new things need to be added?

These plans should be living and adapt to the environment around you. For example, let's say that you set a goal to be promoted and you were. As a result, you are moving to a new city. This is an event-driven reason for renewal. It is the perfect time to reassess your goals. Things that were relevant while you were in the first city may or may not be relevant in your new city.

It is also important to keep your purpose and plans in front of you. Placing your life plan on the refrigerator or your affirmations on your dresser or mirror can keep them in front of you. Try putting a copy of your affirmations on your computer monitor where you will see them every time you log on. All of this is designed to keep your plan alive and healthy.

Summary

The objective of this book has been to provide you with the tools necessary to take control of your life, create your future, and surround yourself with the people and contacts necessary to achieve your life goals. Successfully creating your future requires five things:

Being at cause. Are you happening to life or is life happening to you? Successful people have a mindset toward life that is at cause.

Purpose. Personal purpose provides direction and guides your choices for the future, much like a compass always lets you know which way is north. Successful people have a strong sense of personal purpose.

Plan. Your life plan determines where you are going. Successful people have balanced life plans and measurable achievable goals.

Picture. In order to accomplish your purpose and life plan, you must believe you are capable of accomplishing it. Successful people believe in their abilities to achieve their purpose and life plans.

People. Successful people manage their network of relationships to increase their social capital, thus opening avenues to communication, exposure, and opportunities.

If you completed the exercises in this book, you should have

- a clear understanding of what "being at cause" means,
- a clear purpose for your life,
- a clear plan outlining your goals and a plan to achieve them,
- an understanding of your current self-image,
- definition of the self-image you desire and a plan to achieve it,
- clear definition of your current social network,
- a clear definition of your desired social network, and
- a plan for renewal.

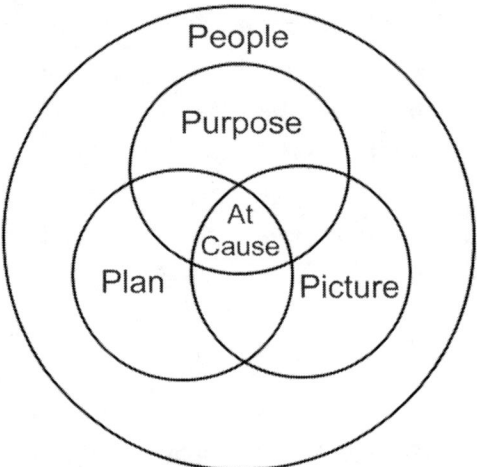

The model is quite simple, but it's a very powerful tool for taking control of your life, creating your future, and surrounding yourself with the people and contacts necessary to successfully achieve your life goals. It helps you make your dash mean what you want it to mean.

Good luck and enjoy the ride!

Life Planning Additional Forms

At Cause:

"I choose to live an at-cause life from this day forth."

Your signature _____

Date ___/___/___

My Purpose:

I choose my unique purpose in life to be

My Plan:

	Needs Improvement	Neutral	Excellent
Physical	(-)	-/+	(+)
Mental	(-)	-/+	(+)
Family	(-)	-/+	(+)
Friends	(-)	-/+	(+)
Money	(-)	-/+	(+)
Work	(-)	-/+	(+)
Religion	(-)	-/+	(+)
Society	(-)	-/+	(+)

My physical health goals

1.

2.

3.

My mental health goals

1.

2.

3.

My family life goals

1.

2.

3.

My friends/social life goals

1.

2.

3.

My money goals

1.

2.

3.

My work life goals

1.

2.

3.

My religious life goals

1.

2.

3.

My society/community life goals

1.

2.

3.

My First Three Actions Steps:

1. _____

2. _____

3. _____

My Picture:

What are the things that I know I can *do* right now that will help me move toward my purpose and goals? How can I capitalize on these things to move me toward my goals?

What are things that I *believe about myself* that will help me move toward my purpose and goals? How can I capitalize on these beliefs to move me toward my goals?

What are the *skills or abilities I need to develop* or find someone to help me with in order to move toward my purpose and goals? What can I do to begin developing these skills and abilities?

What are things that I *believe about myself* that might hinder me from moving toward my purpose and goals? What can I do to challenge these beliefs and replace them with new beliefs that will move me toward my goals?

My Affirmations:

1.

2.

3.

4.

5.

My Social Network:

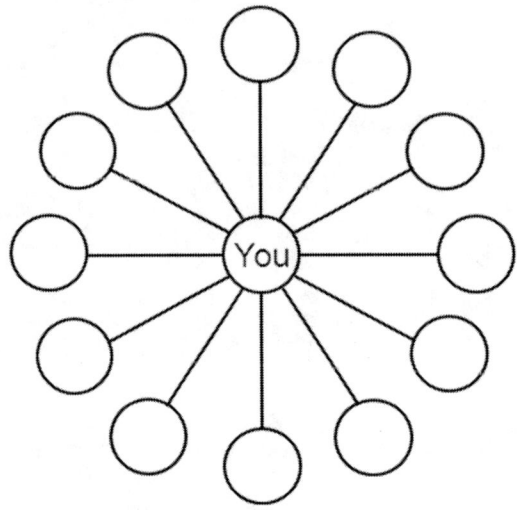

New Network Connections:

How will I introduce myself?	
What do I bring to offer to the relationship?	
What formal organizations do these individuals belong to that I may choose to join?	
What will attract them to me as someone that they would choose to add to their personal relationship network?	
What things do we have in common?	
What things do they like to do?